THE

# cookie sutra

Translated by Edward Jaye

WORKMAN PUBLISHING, NEW YORK

# Dedication

To Lisa for showing me where we keep the baking stuff
and not asking why.

Library of Congress Cataloging-in-Publication Data
Jaye, Edward.
    Cookie sutra / by Edward Jaye.
        p. cm.
    ISBN-13: 978-0-7611-3809-9
    ISBN-10: 0-7611-3809-9
    1. Cookery. 2. Cookery—Humor. 3. Sex—Humor. I. Title.
TX714.J394   2005
613.9'6'0207—dc22                                    2004065913

Cover and book design by Paul Gamarello
Cookies baked by Edward Jaye to be over the age of 21.

Workman books are available at special discounts when purchased in bulk for
premiums and sales promotions as well as for fund-raising or educational
use. Special editions or book excerpts can also be created to specification.
For details, contact the Special Sales Director at the address below.

Workman Publishing Company, Inc.
708 Broadway
New York, NY 10003-9555
www.workman.com
First printing June 2005
10 9 8 7 6 5 4 3 2 1
Printed in Mexico

# The Origins of
# The Cookie Sutra

The art of cooking and the art of love are two of life's
greatest pleasures. Much has been written on both subjects,
but seldom have the two been combined. Until now.
The following pages are part of a manuscript,
which was unearthed in a remote archeological expedition.
The pages were discovered in the kitchen of what
was once the beautiful home of a very wealthy individual.
Almost nothing is known of the original author,
or indeed the date of this ancient text,
but the wisdom contained within is without question.
I have spent the last two years translating this text,
so that others may come to know and understand
the pleasures of *The Cookie Sutra*.

—Edward Jaye

# Getting Ready

## A Recipe for Success

**Preparing the body, preparing the mind, preheating the oven:** One of the greatest luxuries we can afford ourselves is the time to do things right. To let the anticipation and desire build slowly can only increase one's pleasure in the end. Dough needs time to rise, after all. And so do you.

# Bathing

A bath is an excellent way to lose the stresses of daily life and prepare for the pleasures to come. Like climbing into a glass of warm milk, a good bath can work wonders. Even on tough cookies.

# Grooming

The wise gingerbread cookie truly understands the importance of sweetness, and strives to achieve it in all things. After all, if there's one thing a cookie knows, it's how to appear irresistible.

# Perfuming

It is important that you be pleasantly scented for
your partner, as well as pleasing to the eye.
Try something with ginger.
That's a good smell.

# Massage

Also known as "kneading." This tender act may be
entirely innocent, or it can be an exciting way to lead to
something more. The experience may be enhanced by
the use of oils – cooking oil, for example. A good massage
will leave your lover feeling soft and supple as
the day he or she was rolled.

# The Embrace of a Creeper

According to *The Cookie Sutra,* even a simple
embrace can be an effective way to get the molasses
flowing. This embrace has been compared to
the way a serpent, or a vine, winds its way around a
tree. Or the way dough will sometimes stick and wrap
itself around a rolling pin.

# The Kiss That Awakens

There are four main types of kisses: moderate, contracted, pressed, and soft. The kiss that awakens announces your intentions to your partner more clearly than the spoken word. Which is good, because cookies aren't especially big on vocabulary.

# Postures 1
## The Basic Recipes

These simple recipes for lovemaking are
enjoyable for beginners and experts alike.
Try them at home. Or in public.
It is said simple pleasures are best.
They are.

## The First Posture

Often it is the simplest recipes that yield the greatest satisfaction. Like milk and cookies, some classics are tough to beat.

# The Sheep's Posture

According to the *Sutra,* "When the man enters
from behind, his pleasure is increased. When the man
is a gingerbread man, it is doubly so."
This position is a simple way to add variety
and excitement. Not unlike colored sprinkles,
or cinnamon dots.

# Splitting of a Bamboo

Stretching can be an important prelude to sex.
Or if crunched for time, the two may be combined.
But one must not stretch one's partner's leg too
far, for not everyone is a gymnast. Sadly.

# The Pair of Tongs

The accepted wisdom of all cookies states: Everything
is better with a little something on top. As your
confidence in the *Sutra* grows, so too will your enjoyment
of one another. In the bedroom, as in the kitchen, one
should never be afraid to mix things up.

# The Second Posture

As with the first posture, this position is as pleasurable as it
is simple to achieve. Begin as with the first posture
(see page 16), then simply lift and separate.
This position has also been referred to around
the kitchen as "the wishbone."

# The Snake Trap

In this posture each takes a hold of the other,
both promising not to let go until mutual fulfillment
is achieved. In this way the two become as one,
yet the calorie count remains unchanged.

# The Wife of Indra

Not all gingerbread men are created equal.
Named for Indrani, wife of the Hindu God Indra, this
position allows for maximum penetration even if
the gingerbread man is not well endowed.
However, this does make one wonder about
the Hindu God Indra.

# Postures II
## The Advanced Recipes

*The Cookie Sutra* has always maintained that
the greater the challenge, the greater the reward.
Thus the following recipes were created to
stimulate the imagination, stir the senses, and
inflame the appetite.

# The Congress of a Cow

To cookies, cows are sacred. For without them
there would be no milk. It follows then that this position
must be highly pleasurable for it to be so named.
It may not be quite as good as milk, of course.
But then, what is?

# The Ostrich's Tail

To make cookies, dough must first be rolled.
To achieve this position, backs must first be rolled so that
only the woman's head and shoulders are touching down.
With her legs positioned over her partner's shoulders, he
may be tempted to nibble her toes. However,
he must be careful not to take too big a bite, for
that would be wrong.

# Pounding the Spot

Certain texts have referred to this as the greatest
posture of all for mutual gratification. However, this
position does require some degree of flexibility,
and is not easily attained after baking.
Where is "the spot"? Regrettably, some secrets
even cookies will not reveal.

# The Swing

Some ancient texts have referred to this position as one
in which the woman acts the part of a man – but in reality
the woman is in fact acting the part of a swing.
And as everyone knows, swings are fun.

# The Tripod

Many ancient texts speak of the importance of balance
in life. And *The Cookie Sutra* is no exception,
for without balance this position would be impossible.
Beginners may wish to lean on a wall of their
gingerbread house for extra support.

# Rabbit Grooming

Given their reproductive prowess, it's a wonder more positions aren't named for rabbits. This posture requires good leg strength from the woman; however, by rotating her hips a little, she will find the extra effort worthwhile. This posture is also excellent for those who are self-conscious about the faces they make during sex.

# Postures III
## For the Adventurous Cookie

"Where imaginations are fertile,
love will never grow stale."
—an old cookie joke

# The Wheelbarrow

The true practitioner of *The Cookie Sutra* knows inspiration can come anytime, anyplace. Still, our hats are off to whoever first dreamed this up. The Wheelbarrow is an ideal position for those who are intimate, athletic, and on a flat surface.

# Race of the Member

Love is about support, not competition. With this in mind the cookies have managed to concoct a race in which everyone wins. For truly is it written "It's not whether you win or lose, but how you play the game that counts."

# The Suspended Congress

When one is baked light and airy, endless variations
become possible. This congress should first be attempted
with good back support; however, once proficiency is
attained, you may become free to add further movement.
Like jogging.

# Bending the Bow

This position has also been referred to as
"The Rainbow's Arch," in which the man lies at a right
angle to his partner while she holds onto his legs.
It is important to engage in this position slowly and
carefully, however. Otherwise the bow may not be the
only thing that gets bent.

# Scissors

To the inventive cookie even everyday kitchen items hold inspired possibilities. The Scissors, for example, is a highly pleasurable and relatively simple position. Less successful adaptations include such inspired positions as "The Sifter," "The Pastry Bag," and "The Rolling Pin."

# Autumn Dog

As the cookies' experience and expertise in the ways
of the *Sutra* increase, so does the enjoyment in discovering
ever more adventurous ways to share pleasure.
Ultimately, the practitioners will ascend to a higher
level, known as "showing off."

# Afterwards

Having achieved fulfillment, it is time to bask in the
afterglow. Like cookies, everyone needs time to cool down.
This is the moment to relax and let your mind wander
freely. Some think of sleep, and some think of food.
But for the true student of *The Cookie Sutra,* it is time
to pursue life's second greatest passion: baking.
Remembering always that true sweetness
comes from within.

# Bake Your Own Cookie Sutra

(If love has a secret recipe, this is it.)

Yield: About eight 5 x 3 1/2 inch or twenty-four 2 x 1/2 inch
gingerbread men or women

1/2 cup molasses (for a deeper color use blackstrap molasses,
    but be forewarned: it may cut a sweet experience with
    a bitter aftertaste)

2 tablespoons milk

4 tablespoons (1/2 stick) unsalted butter

1/4 cup sugar

2 cups all-purpose flour

1/2 teaspoon baking soda

1 teaspoon ground ginger
    (feel free to add more if you like things spicy)

1 teaspoon ground cloves

1/2 teaspoon ground cinnamon

1/2 teaspoon ground nutmeg

1/2 teaspoon salt

Tube of white icing, colored dragées, and sprinkles, for decorating

1. Preheat the oven to 350°F. Lightly butter 2 cookie sheets.
2. Place the molasses in a heavy saucepan and bring to a boil over medium heat. Stir in the milk.
3. Place the butter and sugar in a mixing bowl. Pour the boiling molasses mixture into the bowl and combine with the butter and sugar until the butter is melted and the mixture is smooth.
4. In a separate bowl, mix together the flour, baking soda, ginger, cloves, cinnamon, nutmeg, and salt. Add in the molasses mixture and combine until the dough comes together. If the dough is too dry, add water 1 tablespoon at a time until it easily forms a ball. If the dough is too wet and sticky, add flour 1 tablespoon at a time and knead until it reaches the right consistency.
5. Remove the dough from the bowl and form it into a ball. Place it on a lightly floured work surface and roll it out to about $1/4$ inch thick.
6. Cut out gingerbread shapes using cookie cutters or free-hand patterns and a sharp knife. Remember, imagination is your ally.
7. Transfer the cookies to the prepared cookie sheets and bake until browned and fragrant, 6 to 8 minutes. Place the cookie sheets on wire racks and allow the cookies to cook for 10 minutes. Then remove the cookies from the sheets to wire racks to finish cooling. Decorate and enjoy, of course.